Club
IMAGINE. BUILD. PLAY.

STEM TRAINING GUIDE BOOK

Guide Book for Teachers, Educators, Homeschoolers and Parents who want to get Started on STEM Teaching. Be the Next-Gen Educator!

Sumita Mukherjee
www.wizkidsclub.com

More books from WIZKIDS CLUB:

Stem/Steam Activity Books: 6-10 Year Kids

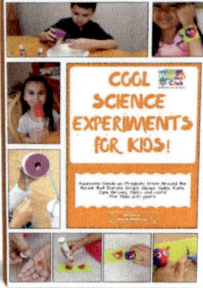

COOL SCIENCE EXPERIMENTS FOR KIDS

Grades: 1-5
Skill level: Beginner
Time: 19 projects; 30-40 minutes each

COOL SCIENCE EXPERIMENTS FOR KIDS is an amazing book full of hands-on activities. With awesome Science, Technology, Engineering, Art and Math project ideas, it is an easy way to entertain any bored kid! A great way to acquire 21st century skills and STEM learning.

Inside this book you will find projects on Simple Machines, Merry-go Round, Spinning Doll, Exploding Bottle, Safe Slime, Architecture, Crafts, Games and more!

Loads of fun with projects that burst, glow, erupt, spin, run, tick and grow!

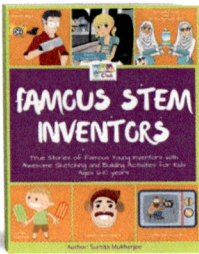

FAMOUS STEM INVENTORS

Grades: 1-5
Skill level: Beginner
Time: Reading time: 15-20 mins and activities of 20-30 minutes each.

FAMOUS STEM INVENTORS introduces kids to the world's most famous young inventors in the field of S.T.E.M. (Science, Technology, Engineering and Math). All things that we enjoy are a product of brilliant minds, scientists and engineers. This book imparts information that is interesting and engaging to young boys and girls between 6-10 years of age.

STORY OF INVENTORS: Kids will be transported to the fascinating world of famous creators and learn about their first inventions: Glowing paper, Popsicle, Windsurf board, Television, Earmuffs and more. The book arouses their natural curiosity to be inspired from their role models.

DESIGN PROCESS: It showcases the Engineering Design Process behind every invention. Highlights what they invented and how they invented, thereby, revealing the steps to all new discoveries.

SKETCHING AND DESIGNING ACTIVITY: It encourages kids to sketch and design their own ideas through the design activity. This book prompts kids to think creatively and it arouses their natural curiosity to build, make and tinker.

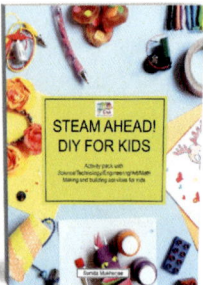

STEAM AHEAD! DIY FOR KIDS

Grades: 1-5
Skill level: Beginner
Time: 21 projects; 30-40 minutes each

STEAM AHEAD! DIY FOR KIDS is an amazing book full of hands-on activities. With awesome Science, Technology, Engineering, Art and Math project ideas, it is an easy way to entertain any bored kid! A great way to acquire 21st century skills and STEM learning.

Inside this book you will find projects on LED cards, dance pads, handmade soaps, bubble blowers, Play-Doh circuits, cloud lanterns, scribbling bots and more!

Awarded 5 stars by READERS' FAVORITE site, Parents, Educators, Bloggers and Homeschoolers.

JOIN THE WIZKIDS CLUB TEAM!

The WIZKIDS CLUB features Highly Engaging Activities, Experiments, DIYs, Travel Stories, Science Experiment Books and more!

Visit www.wizkidsclub.com today!

WizKids Club

IMAGINE. BUILD. PLAY.

www.wizkidsclub.com

TABLE OF CONTENT

ABOUT THE BOOK:

Guide book for teachers, educators, homeschoolers and parents who want to get started on STEM education and teaching. Comprehensive understanding of STEM education.

- What is STEM
- Best practices in STEM
- Growing the maker mindset
- Introducing in classrooms and home
- Inquiry-based teaching
- Engineering design process
- How to make lesson plans
- Tools to make a great STEM lesson plan
- Past, present and future

Get started today and make yourself a next-gen educator!

ABOUT THE AUTHOR:

Sumita Mukherjee is a NASA STEM certified leader and bestselling children's book author. Her books are to inspire young readers to develop a love for discovery and learn about the world around them.

The series of STEAM (Science, Technology, Engineering, Art and Math) and STEM books encourages kids to invent and explore, to empower themselves and see themselves as world leaders and problem solvers. Her books celebrate diversity, spark curiosity and capture children's imaginations!

Her website, WizKidsclub.com was created with a vision to raise the next generation of creative leaders. WizKidsclub offers STEAM programs, educational books, hands-on projects, DIYs, travel stories and engineering books perfect for children 4-12 years.

www.wizkidsclub.com

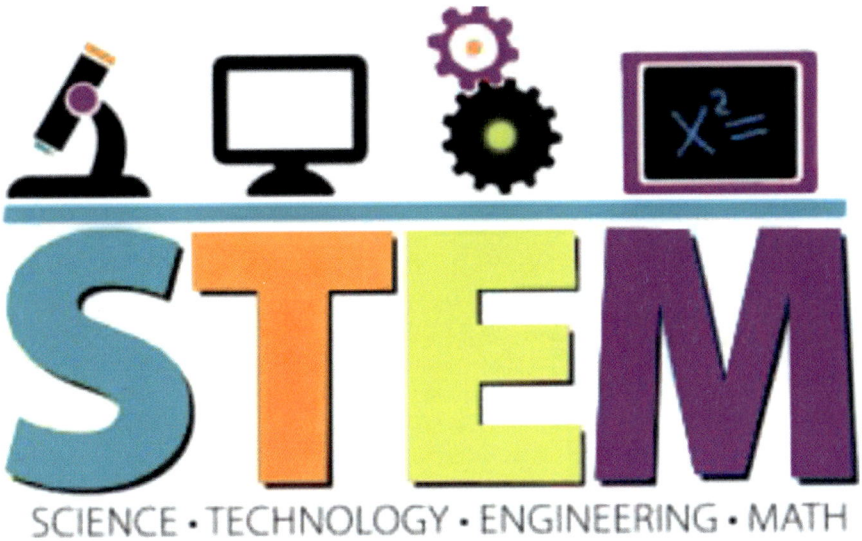

SCIENCE · TECHNOLOGY · ENGINEERING · MATH

CHAPTER 1: Imagine. Build. Play

"In a global economy where the most valuable skill you can sell is your knowledge, a good education is no longer just a pathway to opportunity – it is a prerequisite." Barack Obama.

Wise words from the former president – and more relevant than ever before in the modern world. The point of education is to develop critical thinking, creativity, interpersonal skills and a sense of social responsibility. All these can influence success in life, work and citizenship. A good education is a golden ticket to realms of infinite employment opportunities. Although many traditional job types in today's world are on the decline, there are those which continue to rise. Jobs in industries known as 'STEM industries,' such as computing, engineering and science-based roles, are set to increase by 13% by 2027.

STEM or STEAM is an acronym which stands for Science, Technology, Engineering, Art and Math. Rather than the traditional method of each subject being taught individually and separately at home or in school, STEAM aims to fuse them together into a unified learning model, which is also based on real-life, practical applications.

Our world is becoming increasingly automated and computer-driven as we seek innovations to help us in our busy lives. Needless to say, in order for this to continue, we need more and more graduates in the STEM fields.

Most of our new technology has its basis in science, engineering and mathematics, which is why it is vital to teach children – from an early age – the importance of critical thinking, creativity and understanding of how things work. We do this by introducing hands-on, fun and interactive STEM learning in order to encourage a passion for these subjects. The chart below shows projected STEM careers by 2022.

STEM Career

US-BLS New U.S. STEM Jobs Through 2022 by STEM %

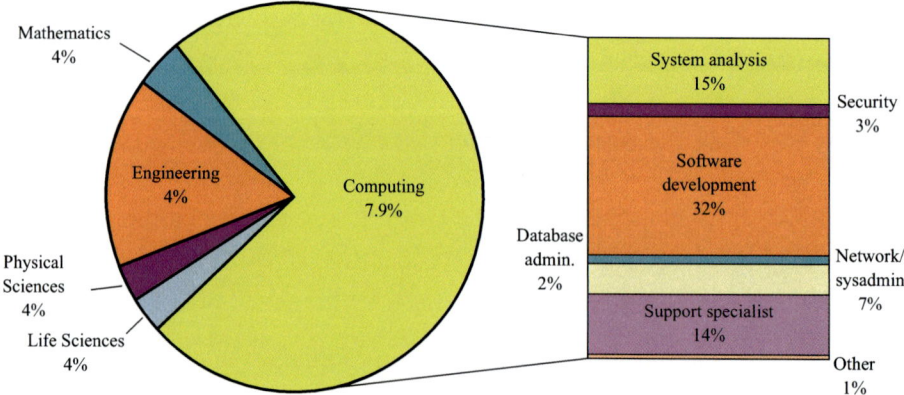

U.S. Commerce Department (2011), Data Source-US-BLS Employment Projection 2012-2022.

CHAPTER 2: All we want for our children is the world

STEAM and STEM learning aims to address a world deficit of expert skills in these vital fields. STEM jobs in computing, engineering and advanced manufacturing are projected to grow by 13% in the year 2027. STEM learning recognizes that teachers, parents and children must tackle a very real shortage of skilled and qualified individuals by making STEM learning accessible, fun and an integral part of school life.

In 2009, President Barack Obama's administration launched a nationwide "Educate to Innovate" campaign in the United States to encourage and motivate students to do exceptionally well in STEAM-related subjects. It is of paramount importance that this important work continues not just in the USA but across the globe.

Future STEM Employment

Recent and Projected Growth in STEM and Non-STEM Employment

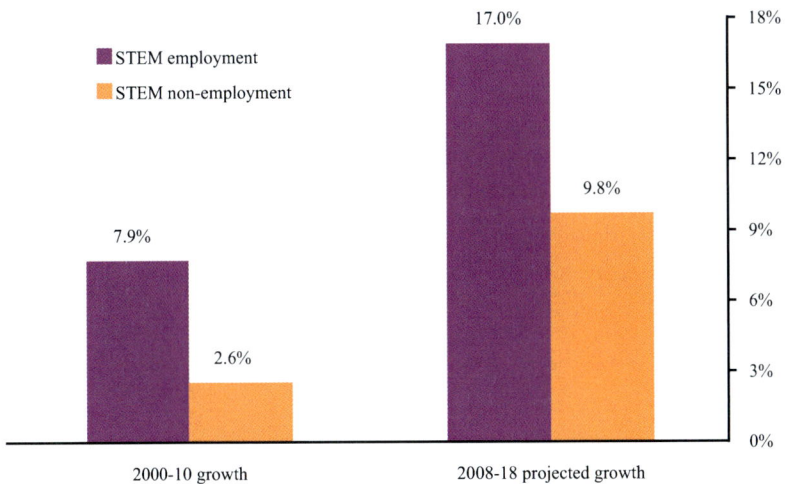

Source: ESA calculation using Current Population Survey public use microdata and estimated from the Employment Projection Program of the Bureau of Labor Statistics.

CHAPTER 3: Around the world with STEM

As awareness of STEM education grows around the world, the following figures from How To STEM give an indication of the current global reach of STEM education.

Australia

When the government-approved National STEM School Education Strategy 2016–2026 was launched, Australia has committed to the development of STEM education by (a) ensuring that all students graduate with a strong foundational knowledge of STEM skills and (b) Ensuring that students are encouraged and inspired to embrace increasingly challenging STEM subjects.

The Australian government has invested $AUD 6 million in its Early Learning STEM Education Scheme (ELSA) and will invest a further $AUD 4 million in its Little Scientists professional development program for educators and teachers of young children, helping to make STEM an integral part of early education.

United Kingdom

In 2016, the Royal Academy of Engineering conducted a report entitled 'UK STEM Education Landscape,' which highlighted the fact that the UK was falling behind in terms of STEM education for young children. Following the report which urged the changing of negative stereotypes regarding certain kinds of jobs and more proactive training of teachers, the Government responded with an acknowledgment of the issue.

Since that time, a number of public and private initiatives have been introduced, including STEM Learning and WISE Campaign. These organizations can approach the Educational Endowment Foundation (EEF), an independent charity which funds innovative educational approaches that have the potential to raise attainment and improve outcomes, for funding. Unfortunately, there are no solid figures regarding projected government spending toward STEM initiatives.

United States

Typically, the United States, a forerunner when it comes to education, recognizes the need for investment in STEM education in order for young people to be competitive in the skilled employment market. In September 2017, President Donald Trump signed a presidential memorandum to expand access to high-quality STEM education for young people. This will put STEM education, particularly computer science, at the forefront of the Department of Education's priorities. The US government also aims to devote at least $200 million a year in grant funds towards STEM-related education.

New Zealand

The New Zealand government is extremely active when it comes to encouraging schools to promote STEM education. This is in direct response to the STEM skills shortage, which, like much of the world, is becoming a growing issue. The Ministry of Education in New Zealand supports teacher training programs such as the Teach First and Manaiakalani Digital Teachers Academy programme which helps to place high-performing STEM graduates and digitally confident teachers in education.In addition, the government has introduced the charmingly named 'A Nation Of Curious Minds' initiative, whose ten-year goal is to promote the importance of science and technology within the education system. Since 2015, the New Zealand government has invested over $NZD 6 million in STEM-based initiatives.

India

In 2015, popular Prime Minister, Narendra Damodardas Modi, launched the 'Skill India' campaign which set out on the ambitious project of training over 400 million youngsters in a number of skills by 2022, skills which are to include STEM subjects. The campaign has, thus far, largely focused on the development of manufacturing innovations and processes for young children. In addition. The India STEM Foundation works in collaboration with India's Department for Science and Technology in order to bring STEM education to the fore. In terms of proactive spend, Australia is shown to be in the lead when it comes to promoting STEM education, but many other countries have proved to have shown vast improvement.

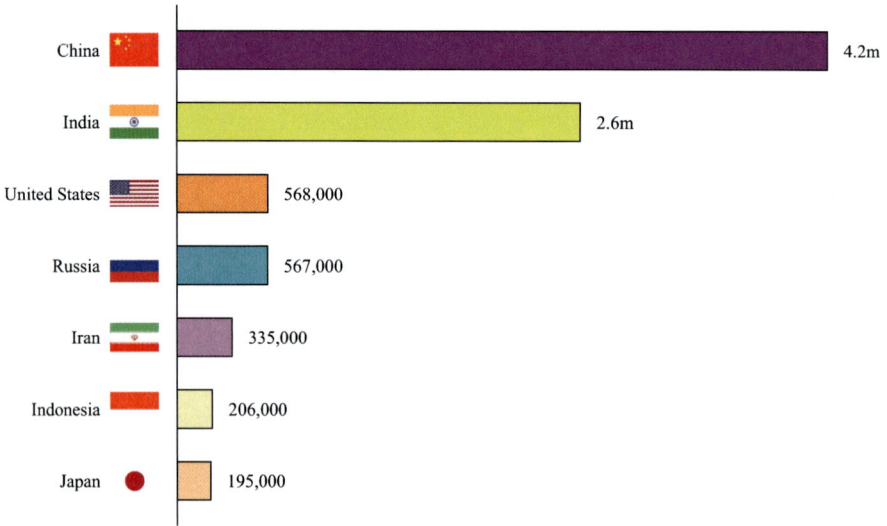

Country	Value
China	4.2m
India	2.6m
United States	568,000
Russia	567,000
Iran	335,000
Indonesia	206,000
Japan	195,000

CHAPTER 4:
WIZKIDSCLUB: Imagine. Build. Play.

A STEAM initiative. Imagined and run by NASA's STEM leader, Sumita Mukherjee, The WIZKIDS CLUB is an initiative designed to help teachers, parents and educators to introduce the fundamentals of STEM and STEAM learning to children aged between 4 and 12 years.

STEM is important. STEM is an economic driver. STEM presents opportunity. We live in a world where national and global societies are dependent on the innovation and creativity of science, technology, engineering, and math (STEM) professionals to improve the conditions of our planet and our quality of life. Despite this, the number of children choosing and graduating with STEM-oriented education is woefully low.

Introducing the Wizkids Club

The WIZKIDS CLUB is dedicated to raising the next generation of creative leaders through STEM learning. Far from the traditional method of classroom teaching, STEM is all about hands-on, practical learning, designed to inspire curiosity and creativity. STEM focuses on computational thinking, finding solutions and answers to real-life problems, and often accentuates learning which is project-based. STEM lessons tend to be exciting and interesting and will include making things and building models. It is important for parents and educators to give their children a chance to tinker, invent, explore and participate in cross-contextual learning.

The Wizkids Club seeks to improve awareness of STEM and STEAM learning through a number of books and workshops by Sumita Mukherjee. It introduces fun and informative ways to approach STEM subjects. Each book is carefully constructed to educate and to encourage children through exciting activities. The STEAM workshops around the world enable kids to enlighten themselves and understand more of science, technology, engineering, art and math.

Workshops in Toronto, Singapore, India, New York, Vietnam have been conducted to spread the joy of STEAM learning.
Visit www.wizkidsclub.com for more information.

Books are the doorway to unlimited knowledge. Wizkidsclub strives to bring the best for kids. For younger children, "Rescue Mission with my STEM Invention" is the ideal book for bringing literature to life for children aged between 6 and 8. Combining a fun story with creativity and science, the book is the perfect way to move your child away from the screen and into a lifelong love of reading and sparking creative ideas.

This book tells the story of Tiffany, Nicole and Alan, a group of children who are excited about being entered into the annual Best Tech Idea contest. Three brilliant middle school STEMists, they proudly present their "Forever Slime Soap," "Oxygen Producing Motor," "Oil Sucking Contraption" and "Colour Changing Cake" – a piece of cake for top STEMists like these three – but someone's out to ruin their chances!

In addition to the books, the Wizkids Club offers useful resources, lesson plans and after school club ideas for teachers and educators. For more, check out www.wizkidsclub.com

NEXT-GEN STEM\STEAM BOOKS: K-5 YEAR OLD KIDS

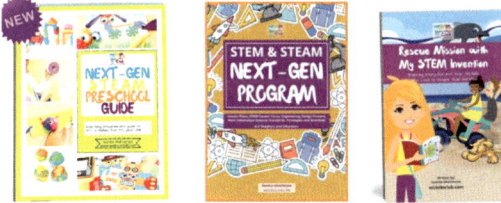

STEM\STEAM ACTIVITY BOOKS: 6-10 YEAR KIDS

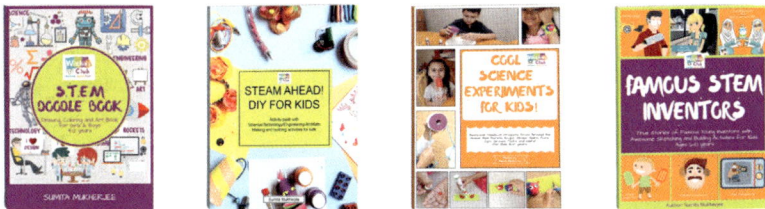

ENGINEERING & DIY BOOKS: 6-10 YEAR KIDS

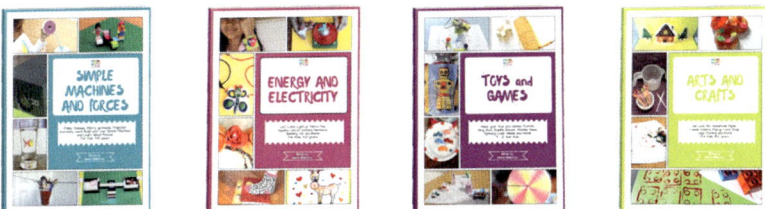

CHAPTER 5: The reality of STEM

I want us all to think about new and creative ways of engaging young people in science and engineering, whether through science festivals, robotics competitions, fairs that encourage young people to create, build and invent….to be "makers of things; not just consumers of things": President Barack Obama

These words are particularly important in a world where young people are heavily influenced by the lives of participants in reality TV shows. A study published by The Independent shows that 1 in 10 teenagers say that they would be happy to abandon their education for the chance to earn fame and fortune as a
reality TV star.

Helping engage students in STEM subjects is of vital importance as worldwide figures show a need for millions more employees in this field. As with anything worthwhile, this will take investment. Current studies reveal that less than 50% of students show a very real interest in these subjects worldwide, with many choosing not to pursue them. There are, however, exceptions:

In 2014, 13-year-old David Cohen of Minnesota was a finalist in the Discovery Education 3M Young Scientist Challenge. Although David has worked on several projects, he was recognized for the creation of a robot modeled on an earthworm's musculatory system, with the aim of preventing diseases associated with mosquitos by eliminating immature ones.

On being asked about the people David credits with his success, he replied, "I credit a lot of people. I credit my parents; my mentor, Dr. Langer-Anderson; my science teachers and really even my friends who have supported me through this entire process."

David's story is a prime example of students pursuing a passion for STEM subjects and creating real-world tools.

How do we encourage more David Cohens?

When it comes to populating the STEM genre of jobs, some of the challenges which have been identified include:

- A need to attract more female candidates
- A need to attract more candidates from minority groups
- A need to establish the relevance of STEM subjects to students in line with their existing interests
- A need to differentiate between jobs with STEM titles and those jobs with non-STEM titles which incorporate some or all of the same skills.

In order to create and encourage the innovators of tomorrow, experts say that we need more than financial investment. Blair Blackwell, the manager of Education and Corporate Programs at Chevron Corporation, has stated that a much more involved and hands-on approach is required. "From a business standpoint, this is not just about writing a check," Blackwell says. "It's investing, but also being a hands-on partner for providing solutions and coming together to ensure all our students … have opportunities to be tomorrow's innovators."

Mirroring Blackwell's words, David Cohen credits his mentor and his science teachers with inspiring him to work on his STEM inventions.

It has been demonstrably proven that young children can be encouraged to embrace the sciences through the introduction of fun and interactive projects but, despite this, science is currently taught in most schools for less than three hours a week. Studies suggest that this is due to more focus being put on the high-stakes testing subjects. It's also shown that children are mainly memorizing information when studying science which accounts for the lack of passion in the subject.

By changing the way science and technology is taught, we change the way children react to these subjects.

CHAPTER 6: Best ways to spread the love for STEM

1. Mentoring in schools

The NSW Department of Education has established seven STEM Action Schools to mentor and share innovative STEM practice and programs with schools. STEM Action Schools implement curriculum programs designed to develop students' foundational knowledge and skills in STEM subjects as well as skills of collaboration, critical and creative thinking, and problem-solving. This is, of course, fantastic for those able to attend a STEM Action School, but what about those attending ordinary schools?

In an ideal world, a teacher of STEM subjects can become a mentor to gifted and passionate children. Unfortunately, in reality, time and budget constraints mean that this is rarely possible. Instead, teachers can encourage tomorrow's innovators by putting them in touch with a mentor program.

2.Local Business

Many companies and organizations are more than willing to get involved in STEM education by mentoring their future employees. As well as targeting their future workforce, mentoring students help businesses to connect with a local community on a very real level. Teachers looking for mentors for their students can consult with school administrators for existing lists of such companies. If a school does not have an existing list, the local chamber of commerce will be happy to supply one.

3. Students In Further Education

Who better to mentor a student than one who has recently been in their shoes? Most colleges and universities have engineering, science and technology departments packed full of enthusiastic students who have actively chosen those subjects. Most Deans and Professors will be happy to speak to teachers looking for student mentors and will often help to connect mentors to students. One major benefit of this is that many younger students look up to teens who have achieved that mysterious level between child and adult and so will thrive under their mentorship. ls to explain how the company works, why it's important, and how students like themselves are an integral part of the company's future.

4. Industrial Action

As well as schools providing mentors for young STEM enthusiasts, a very effective method of creating a buzz about STEM subjects in students is to involve the very companies which may end up employing them. A great example of this is the worldwide technology company, Cubic, who has shown an outstanding commitment to STEM education. Cubic's motto is "Success through innovation in technology, processes and services delivery is both our proud history and our calling for the future." Putting its money where its mouth is, Cubic shows its commitment by participating in a wide range of projects and events every year, including San Diego's Festival of Science & Engineering, the Team America Rocketry Challenge, and many more. In addition to a presence at important STEM events, Cubic organizes school visits during which representatives of the company visit schools to explain how the company works, why it's important, and how students like themselves are an integral part of the company's future. Tackling the dual challenges of providing mentors and encouraging more female interest in STEM is Million Women Mentors – a movement which connects mentor volunteers in STEM occupations with students. Recognizing that young women often look for role models as their interests and skills develop, Million Women Mentors aims to increase confidence as well as offer opportunities within science, technology, engineering and math.

"Keep exploring. Keep dreaming. Keep asking why. Don't settle for what you already know. Never stop believing in the power of your ideas, your imagination, your hard work to change the world."

5. Remote Mentoring

Often, the location of the STEM student means that 'real life' mentors may not be readily available. In these instances, there are a number of options for remote mentoring, including online resources. There are a number of online organizations who can organize safe and free interaction through a secure site between mentor and mentee. Although the mentors are often university and college students, in some cases, mentors working in a student's intended profession are available.

CHAPTER 7: Growing the maker mindset

Although it's important for schools to lead the way when it comes to pushing STEM to the forefront of education, a real STEM journey begins long before a child is of school age. Parents of young children need to instill in their offspring a passion and curiosity about the world they live in, in order to prepare them for their school years.

The good news for parents is that there are a great number of resources available to help them steer their budding STEMmers in the right direction.

1. STEM Learning Centers

Many may be surprised to learn that the first step on the STEM is an activity which their young child is probably already involved in – building. Many toys and games for young children involve the development of building skills, such as Lego and sticklebricks. Creating STEM learning centers at home can be a great start. Parents can capitalize on these fun toys by introducing a more structured form of building in order to show children that they can actually build something useful.

The purpose of STEM education is to allow young people to investigate their world in terms of different settings – in practice, this works through simple exercises such as turning an activity like collecting seashells into a mathematical exercise (How many did we find? How many are white?). This can be applied to toys like Lego as simply as encouraging a child to count the bricks.

You can introduce very young children to the concept of building using simple household objects such as plastic cups, inner tubes from kitchen and toilet rolls, and boxes. To add fun for the child, you can use candy to create a stimulating project with the added bonus of a treat at the end such as jelly bean building whereby several jelly beans are attached together with toothpicks to demonstrate how construction is completed by joining things together.

2. Through Books and Stories

For parents of young children, there are countless books available to help with inspiration for STEM building projects. Some of the books I've found useful are as follows:

Make: Paper Toys And Play Pack introduces young children to the concept of making something for real-life use. Full of easy to follow instructions, the book shows parents and children how to make simple items such as hats and decorations for a birthday party.

Simple Machines & Forces for grades 1 to 5 is a treasure chest of building projects including simple machines, such as a seesaw and a shoebox projector, that actually work.

The Engineering Activity Book puts together a number of simple building projects and lots of fun facts to engage a child's imagination.

STEM Activity: Sensational Science is a great introduction to the world of science for young children. As well as learning about the world we live in, children can get involved by building models of atoms, planets and more to encourage a more hands-on understanding.

Next-Gen S.T.E.A.M Preschool Guide is the perfect companion for parents of young children. Packed with 40 easy projects, the book covers building as well as science and technology.

All children love stories and, Rescue Mission With My STEM Invention is a great way to fire a child's imagination as they follow the adventures of the children in the story as they prepare to enter an invention competition.

3. Workshops and events

As well as these great books, parents committed to their child's STEM education can attend a variety of workshops – many of which can be a fun day out for parents and children as well as an educational one.

The WizKids Club workshops offer toy and card making, simple robotics and many other activities within a fun and safe environment.

Fizzicks Education holds a number of workshops, parties and other events throughout the year as well as its great website offering blog posts, shopping and 100 free experiments. It's a good idea to get in touch with your local authority in order to find out what's available in your area. Most authority's education departments will hold a list of events and resources that are available.

Should you find that you're unable to get to a workshop, there are a number of online resources such as Pre-school Plan. It offers online workshops for parents and teachers.
https://www.preschool-plan-it.com/online-preschool-workshops-store.html

Another great resource is the STEM From The Start site for parents and teachers, offering lessons and practical advice on STEM education. *stemfromthestart.org*

Why not set up your own STEM workshop if there isn't an existing one in your area? This handy guide can help you to set up an after-school club or workshop in your area for interested students.

https://www.stem.org.uk/sites/default/files/pages/downloads/STEM-Clubs-handbook.pdf

For further inspiration, check out some of the women leading the way in STEM education HERE.

https://www.rolls-royce.com/country-sites/sea/discover/2017/women-leading-the-way-in-stem.aspx

CHAPTER 8: STEM
in the classroom

The Benefits of STEM explained:

How does STEM benefit elementary lessons? This is a question that's asked a lot by people who believe that STEM subjects are too complex for elementary students. This is very much not the case – introducing STEM activities (and STEAM) into the lessons of elementary students is a lot less daunting than it sounds. In fact, creating STEM activities and lesson plans brings benefits to all students, at all ages and abilities, promoting a positive, inclusive and effective educational opportunity.

When it comes to introducing STEM activities and programs, it really is never too early; in fact, creating a love for these subjects from a young age ensures a continued passion as the children get older.

IF EDUCATION DESTROYS A STUDENT'S LOVE OF LEARNING, THEN IS IT WORKING OKAY?
In the modern world, the ability to continually evolve and learn is absolutely paramount for success. There really are so few areas of our world which are not constantly changing due to technology that not instilling a love of learning and exploration is really doing the student a disservice.

THE GREATEST BENEFIT OF STEM EDUCATION IS THAT IT FOSTERS A PASSION FOR LEARNING DURING THE IMPORTANT ELEMENTARY YEARS.
Think about how excited about the world very young children are, and then compare that to their reluctance to learn after a few years at school.

We need to ask ourselves what it is about the school system that knocks the love of learning out of our children.

IF THEY ARE LEARNING TO HATE LEARNING AT SCHOOL, IT'S

THE SCHOOL THAT'S AT FAULT!
So, what can we do? We can ensure that from the elementary school stage, learning continues to be fun and engaging and focused on a child's natural curiosity. We also need to instill confidence in learning through hands-on STEM methods.

BUT MOST OF THESE STUDENTS AREN'T GOING TO BECOME SCIENTISTS.
It's easy to buy into the common misconception that STEM is only for super-smart science students. In fact, STEM is for everyone – it's not about becoming a scientist but about learning to apply STEM subjects to everyday life, no matter what profession the child chooses. For example, baking employs a number of STEM subjects including chemical reactions, digital tools, and a form of engineering in the way that a cake or other food items are shaped during cooking. Baking can also include the arts in terms of decoration and presentation. This is just one example of STEM being used in everyday life.

HOW CAN STEM LEARNING IN ELEMENTARY CREATE A LOVE OF LEARNING?
A quality STEM program should provide the following benefits: Motivation, engagement, and real-world inspired subjects. Knowledge should be taught the way it is used in the real world, with concepts and subjects interwoven seamlessly. Students become involved in integrated projects and apply meaningful and important content.

Everything taught and learned is useful and can be applied in the real world. Students are fully engaged, leading to a greater understanding of the concepts.

STEAM is creative and adaptable, making it accessible to children of every ability level as they learn to work together as a team. Rather than traditional textbook teaching, STEM is all about the student and is designed to fire up his or her curiosity and creative thought process. Lessons incorporate real-life activities that a student can relate to and provide students with ownership over their learning. Teamwork, collaboration and communication are a major focus. Students are encouraged to be creative in their thinking and to suggest different ways of achieving a result. Students understand that it's OK if a project doesn't work the first time around.

The value of failure as a learning opportunity is emphasized and mistakes are embraced instead of penalized. STEAM embraces the 4 C's which are identified as key 21st-century skills – Creativity, Collaboration, Critical Thinking, and Communication.

STEM lessons are an excellent way of reducing classroom anxiety by reducing the stress of right and wrong answers in traditional learning. Seeing STEM in practice is the best way to understand the importance – the success – of this method of learning.

CHAPTER 9: Inquiry-based STEM teaching methods

Inquiry-based teaching strategies are a really powerful tool for educators looking to connect with their students through STEM principles. Although some students may struggle with the free-form nature that STEAM learning can take, as an educator, you should be able to reassure these students. The lack of structure can be intimidating and strange for those used to the step-by-step nature normally used to teach school topics. For students new to this type of learning, keep in mind the 4 different types of inquiry instructions and use the one most appropriate for your students, project and situation.

STRUCTURED INQUIRY METHOD

This is the term used to describe the method which is most similar to traditional teaching. In this method, the teacher leads the students through a work process as a class. The teacher will explain the project, distribute the materials and provide detailed instructions on how the project should be completed. The goal here is for the teacher to move the learning toward a more student-focused approach where students take greater control over the project and processes.

CONTROLLED INQUIRY METHOD

This is the term for a framework whereby the teacher provides the context and goals along with a few ideas before allowing the students to pilot the project themselves. Although the students can, of course, ask the teacher for advice, they are encouraged to work together as a team to find solutions themselves.

GUIDED INQUIRY METHOD

This is the term used for the process whereby a teacher chooses a topic or questions and then invites the students to develop their own lines of inquiry and investigation. The students will work as a team to decide what materials they need and what they need to do in order to complete the project.

FREE INQUIRY METHOD

Possibly a little daunting for some teachers new to STEM teaching, in the Free Inquiry Method, the students are able to choose the project from an umbrella list and then explore and complete it in whatever way they see fit. It's a good idea to leave this one until students are accustomed to student-led learning.

LEARNING HOW TO IMPLEMENT IN-QUIRY-BASED LEARNING IS KEY TO SUCCESS

Teachers must not expect children to intuitively know how to be self-motivated learners or to necessarily welcome the freedom of this kind of learning. As the teacher, start slowly and make it clear that you are always there to support and help students. Sometimes, just becoming comfortable with new processes or learning techniques is the most important lesson of all. Self-confidence in one's ability to learn something is the key to empowering a student to become a lifelong learner. Never underestimate the importance of spending time teaching children how to learn, how to take ownership of their learning, and also how to work as a team.

Note the difference between working as a team whereby each member has a role according to their strengths and working as a group which is a less-structured way of working.

CHAPTER 10: The Engineering Design Process

In order to engage your students in engineering, the only prerequisite is a desire to lead them on problem-solving adventures. Each student may attack a problem differently and projects may or may not be successful depending on the approach taken. The end result, however, is that your students will be engaged, apply their learning in creative ways, develop their analytic and problem-solving skills, and be excited about learning!

To help you design an engineering project, here are four main steps to keep in mind:

1) Define a Problem

The first step is to define a real-world problem that meets your standards and content requirements, has many grade-appropriate pathways to success, and can be understood by students. The problem can lead to a process or a product solution as both are vital to the work of engineers.

2) Identify what is required in order to solve the problem

What is it that you want your students to be able to achieve before, during, and after the engineering design project? If your students are creating a process for purifying a large water source, they must be able to understand the physical and chemical properties of water and solutions; be able to work as a team to design, test, and re-design a process based on their knowledge; and be able to present and defend their findings to others. Engineering projects harness students' knowledge of science and math and technology as well as learning new things. There needs to be a focus on collaborative skills, metacognition (the art of self-thinking and regulation), resiliency, and perseverance.

Once you've chosen your performance criteria, you can then design processes and checklists which will form the project plan for students.

3) Design Activities

This is where you and your students' creativity comes into play; it is the beauty of STEM. In order to pose an engaging and fun problem, look at the following questions:
- What is the problem being posed?
- Which STEM standards (NGSS, CCSSM, ISTE) does your problem align with?
- What kind of background information will your students need in order to solve the problem?
- What kind of limits and constraints will the students have (i.e. time, material, budget, etc.)?
- How will your students collaborate to solve the problem?
- How will your students gather, test and evaluate their products/solutions before redesigning?
- How will students share their results?

4) Training Student-Engineers

You don't want to set your students up to fail, so you need to apply some training before setting them off on their project. It's also really important to allow enough time for students to test their solutions, collaborate and communicate with each other, and then make the necessary revisions to their solutions. Try the following tips:

- Make sure that expectations and ground rules for group work are made clear and that students know how to set up and clean up a project, and how they are expected to communicate.
- Assign student roles for the group work and provide students with plenty of time and opportunity to practice their roles.

- Incorporate enough time within the project for students to test their solutions, share their results with the group, answer any questions, and receive constructive criticism on the design – explain to them how these kinds are essential to the job of an engineer.
- Allow plenty of time for students to modify and improve their solutions based on their test results and feedback – a failure in many cases is just one step to a better solution!
- Make appropriate reading material and diagrams available to all students at all times.

Implementing these new engineering processes and disciplines in your classroom will, of course, take some time and a shift in practices, but the value to your students and to you, as a teacher, will be well worth the effort!

CHAPTER 11: STEM lesson plans and activities

Although it may seem complex, to begin with, once you begin to apply STEM principles in the classroom, it will soon become second nature as you and your students explore STEM together. Before you know it, Science, Technology, Engineering, Math and the Arts will become integrated into much of your teaching.

We've discussed the benefits of various STEM lessons and activities, the value of inquiry-based teaching methods and the Engineering Design process. Now, we know the value of STEM, but how do we create STEM lesson plans? For many teachers, it can seem really complicated, but we promise it's not – especially if you follow our these simple steps.

CREATING STEM LESSON PLANS:

So, what does STEM education look like? Once you start looking for ways to enhance your lessons with STEM, you will realize just how easy it is to create interdisciplinary activities that really engage your students.

Your first step to getting started with STEM is to develop your lessons and activities. A history lesson can quickly and easily be transformed into a STEM lesson with just a few changes to the focus. Similarly, a study of Ancient Egypt becomes an engineering, science and math challenge by tasking your students with designing catapults. Suddenly, your simple lesson is a full STEAM activity using all the pillars of Science, Technology, Engineering, Arts and Math.

1. Does my STEM lesson need to have an engineering approach as a framework for the lesson? This is non-negotiable for STEM lessons. The engineering design process (EDP) provides an organized approach to solving STEM challenges. The "E" in STEM forms the key difference between traditional lessons and STEM lessons. Note, however, that your lesson doesn't necessarily have to follow the steps of the EDP too rigidly.

2. Does my STEM lesson have to apply actual math and science content through authentic student experiences? Does your lesson incorporate the objectives that your students are learning in any given quarter? This helps students to better understand why you are doing certain things in order to complete these projects. Within your STEM lesson, try to connect the math and science contents. You may need to collaborate with other math or science teachers to get full insights into how these can be integrated.

3. Does my STEM lesson deal with real-world issues and problems? This is, basically, the fundamental core of STEM lessons. They need to address real social, economic, and environmental situations in a way that students can relate to.

4. Do my STEM lessons encourage hands-on inquiry and open-ended exploration? STEM teachers use inquiry-based, firsthand projects which encourage critical thinking, problem-solving, and teamwork. The lessons should not be prescriptive. Do not give your students step-by-step instructions to follow in order to reach an answer or solution. Children should have plenty of opportunities to explore and discover their own possible solutions.

5. Do my STEM lessons allow for more than one correct answer? In STEM lessons, it must be stressed that there is no single right answer. STEM challenges generally have several possible right solutions. To reiterate a point made in #4: Allow your students plenty of freedom to do their own research, explore various possibilities, and generate ideas for solutions.

6. Do my STEM lessons encourage students to work in teams? Productive teamwork is an important skill that the children we teach will need in the 21st-century workforce. Separate students into teams to communicate, think together, share ideas, and develop solutions. My STEM lessons also include tips for helping students to work together successfully in teams.

7. Do I have the right scenario to introduce the problem – particularly for elementary and middle school students? Scenarios are there to set the stage and pique kids' interest. You can come up with your own scenario or locate one on the Web: http://www.egfi-k12.org. What I like about this site is that, following each scenario, the narrator identifies several different problems that the teams could choose to solve. I generally use the scenario to introduce the particular problem they are going to solve. However, letting them select from a menu of problems will ensure more student choice and buy-in.

8. Does my lesson put the teacher in a facilitator role rather than a lecture/ discussion role? Remember to write your lessons in such a manner that they minimize the risk of a teacher just standing in front of students and telling them what they need to know. The teacher should explain, monitor, support, and oversee the work of her student teams. She or he should leave space open for the students to learn and make decisions themselves.

9. Do my STEM lessons engage my students in communicating during and after the project? Accurate and useful communication is an extremely important workforce skill and can take place in a number of different ways. Students may communicate with experts during their quest for a solution. They may regularly communicate with other teams to exchange information. They may publicize their final solutions in writing, online, through drama processes, or in other ways. Give them options for their expression and communication.

10. Do my STEM lessons remove the fear of failure? Do they help students and teachers understand that failure is a positive step toward discovering and creating a solution and is, in fact, a necessary step in learning and designing solutions? During STEM lessons, all students should feel safe in taking risks. Mistakes can actually lead them to a deeper level of understanding.

11. Do my STEM lessons appeal equally to boys and girls? All STEM lessons need not deal directly with machinery. Some might spotlight health or environmental issues that appeal to a wide variety of students. STEM lessons should also involve special education students in experiencing success.

12. Do my STEM lessons promote authentic assessments in determining student and team success? For example, you may suggest that teachers give teams rubrics to help them determine the degree to which their products meet the criteria and constraints. Teamwork productivity can and should be evaluated. Project participation should be high for all students as well as equal where possible. Scores on math and science contents should increase. Come up with multiple ways to assess students, and this shouldn't start and end with multiple choice tests.

CHAPTER 12: 6 ways to make an amazing STEM Lesson

I hope these guidelines help you to collaborate with other teachers and create lessons which apply technology to what students are learning in science and math as well as other
subjects.

1. STEM lessons should focus on real-world issues and challenges. In STEM lessons, students address real-world social, economic, and environmental problems and seek solutions. My biggest STEM success moment came when I moved to a new role and, for the first time, faced a class of science students who had given up on school. I had the class identify a real-world problem and suddenly I found I had a class of engaged students who were enthused over a STEM project — before the familiar acronym had even burst onto the scene.

2. STEM lessons should be guided by the engineering design process. The EDP provides a flexible process that takes students from identifying a problem — or a design challenge — to creating and developing a solution. If you search for "engineering design process images" online, you'll find a number of charts to guide you, but most have the same basic steps as suggested previously. In this process, students define problems, conduct background research, develop multiple ideas for solutions, develop and create a prototype, and then test, evaluate, and redesign them.

    This is a bit like the scientific method, but during the EDP, teams of students try their own research-based ideas, attempt different approaches, make errors, accept and learn from them, and try again. Their focus is on developing solutions.

3. STEM lessons should immerse students in real hands-on.

4. STEM lessons should involve students in productive teamwork. Helping students inquiry and open-ended exploration. In STEM lessons, the path to learning is extremely open-ended, within necessary constraints. Constraints generally involve things like available materials. The students' work is hands-on and collaborative, and decisions about solutions are student-generated. Students need to communicate to share ideas and redesign their prototypes as needed. They control their own ideas and design their own investigations. work together as a productive team is never an easy job. It becomes exponentially easier if all STEM teachers at a school work together to implement teamwork, using the same language, procedures, and expectations for students.

5. STEM lessons apply rigorous math and science content to what your students are learning. In your STEM lessons, you should always purposely connect and integrate content from selected math and science courses. Plan to collaborate with other math and/or science teachers in order to gain insight into how course objectives can be interwoven in a given lesson. Students are then able to see that science and math are not isolated subjects but can connect to solve problems. This adds relevance to their math and science learning. In STEM, students can also use technology in appropriate ways to design their own products (also technologies). Best case scenario: involve an art teacher as well. Art, surprisingly, plays a critical role in product design. Teams will want their products to be attractive, appealing, and marketable. When the arts are added, the STEM acronym becomes STEAM.

6. STEM lessons allow for multiple correct answers and turn failure into a necessary part of learning. Sometimes, I designed my science labs so that all the teams would replicate the same results or verify or refute a hypothesis. Students were studying specific science contents and the whole idea was to provide insight into cause and effect by manipulating variables. STEM classes, by contrast, always provide opportunities for many different right answers and approaches. The STEM environment offers rich possibilities for creative solutions. When designing and testing prototypes, teams may flounder and fail to solve the problem. That's okay. They are expected to learn from what went wrong and try again. Failure is considered a positive step on the way to discovering and designing solutions.

CHAPTER 13: Creating STEM lesson plans

1) Understanding and Practicing the Engineering Design Process:

It's vital to know the engineering design process well and to incorporate it into lessons which harness and develop 21st-century skills. Work out methods and strategies to incorporate makerspaces within the school library and classrooms. A good way to start can be to get on an engineering design challenge of designing a roller coaster marble run using recycled materials, or designing and creating a vehicle which is powered by air. It could also be to design and build a Vibrobot, etc. These can be great places to start your self-training and implementation of your learning.

2) Get to know the latest in classroom technology and products:

Familiarize yourself with all of the technology, tools and kits which are commonly used in school libraries and classrooms. Makerspaces include Makey Makey, Snap Circuits, LittleBits, Makedo, Ozobot, Fisher Price Code-A-Pillar, Squishy Circuits, and more. I have added a bit more on the latest technologies below. Analyze a toy or household gadget. Take the gadget apart, and identify and label the parts.

Brainstorm how the components from the deconstructed broken gadgets can be used to create new gadgets and inventions or used to repair similar gadgets. Continue self-training by conducting building engineering challenges and robotics. STEM is making its way into afterschool programs. Find out low-cost technology that can be incorporated within the early childhood / elementary classroom on a daily basis. Many of these tools can be incorporated within the block center, such as levels, rulers, tape measures, and journaling.

3) Teaching STEM using Children's Literature:

Explore STEM-based children's titles which are ideal for incorporating STEM into lessons. Titles include many from the NSTA list of Outstanding STEM Trade Books for 2017-2018. Check out *wizkidsclub.com/books* for more books on STEM and STEAM.

Investigate how these books can be incorporated into the lesson plans. Include lots of hands-on-minds-on, inquiry-based STEM investigations during this process; from materials science, to reverse engineering, engineering journaling, and exploring electricity-based kits and more.

A good example of a theme is "Studying the Human Skeleton," which introduces project-based learning through the medium of story, with a wide-array of exploratory centers which can be incorporated within the classroom environment to investigate the human skeleton in-depth. In addition, connections are made across the disciplines to include art, engineering, physical education, math, reading and writing. You could also re-design existing lesson plans to be more project-based.

Explore a number of different concepts via a guided-inquiry approach. You can explore the following concepts: structure and function, biomimicry, chemistry, super absorbing polymers, plant and animal cells, force, motion, energy concepts, simple machines, aeronautical concepts, and more through storybooks and STEM next-gen books.

4) Exploring Science, Technology, Engineering, and Math (STEM) Practices and Content at home:

Ordinary household objects and mathematical tools such as rulers, spirit levels and measuring tapes can be incorporated to conduct projects and experiments.

During the fun and often enlightening exploration, you could work on a number of projects including:

- Exploring the way things work by analyzing simple gadgets.
- Predicting what the interior of a gadget will look like and how it works – they will draw the gadget, then take it apart and put it back together.
- Exploring force, motion, and energy concepts through the conducting of experiments with toys.
- Designing, constructing and testing an air-powered car made from recycled materials.
- Conducting explorations to determine what shapes and designs tend to make the strongest structures.
- Exploring aeronautical, force, motion, and energy concepts by designing, building and testing a variety of paper model helicopters.
- Designing, constructing and testing model parachutes.
- Exploring force, motion, energy, aeronautical, and engineering concepts as they conduct experiments with store-bought airplanes and paper model airplanes.
- Exploring the field of solar energy by designing, constructing, and testing solar ovens.

5) Incorporating the Arts into STEM: From STEM to STEAM

Although STEM subjects are necessary for scientific and technological progress, without the arts, it is impossible for students to become fully engaged to reach their full potential. This is because art and design subjects give students the freedom to be creative and enjoy the capabilities and potential of STEM. The figures collected from numerous studies already paint a grim future for STEM subjects and careers in the United States. The relevance of art subjects cannot be emphasized enough. Various independent studies have revealed that art students have a much better chance of being recognized for their academic achievement. Furthermore, art students have a higher likelihood of receiving school attendance awards. This shows that art students are self-driven and motivated in their studies. Actively explore a number of projects like:

- STEM-based art projects
- Thought-provoking art explorations
- Role-playing
- Question and answer sessions

Training and studying of the arts help your students to build vital interpretative skills. This goes a long way toward developing a student's creativity. When STEM is successfully combined with some art studies through mutually reinforced objectives, students can learn both areas easily. This is because the arts infuse creativity and interest into a student's learning process. Studying art-related subjects contributes to the development of essential skills like cross-cultural, social, problem-solving, and critical thinking. It also enhances a student's flexibility, adaptability, creativity, and innovation. All these skills are required for a successful career in any field of study. Therefore, you should consider incorporating arts into the STEM lesson plans.

6) Green Engineering: Implementing Socially and Globally Responsible Engineering Challenges in the Classroom

Environmental engineers take on various roles, including environmental cleanup, water quality, groundwater resources, surface water and groundwater flow, water contamination, waste disposal, and air pollution. The national and regional curriculum ensures that students are aware of the standards.

Basically, students should learn about the different factors which affect water quality and the conditions which enable different animals and plants to survive in their environments. After this, students become aware of groundwater and how environmental engineers study groundwater to predict the distribution of surface pollution.

Students also learn how water flows through the ground, what an aquifer is, and what soil properties are used to predict groundwater flow. Additionally, students discover that the water they drink every day comes from many different sources, including surface water and groundwater. They will investigate possible scenarios of drinking water contamination and how these contaminants can negatively affect the organisms that come in contact with them. Students learn about the three most common methods of waste disposal and how environmental engineers continue to develop different technologies to dispose of trash.

Finally, students learn the causes of air pollution and how to investigate the different pollutants that exist, such as toxic gases and particulate matter. Also, they investigate the technologies developed by engineers to reduce air pollution.

Engineers, in their various roles, continually work to prevent pollution so that our air is safe to breathe and our water is safe to drink and use for bathing and recreating. Different types of engineers continue to explore new, creative ideas to lower harmful air emissions, such as designing more efficient vehicles, industrial filters to reduce the amount of particulate matter released into the atmosphere, and indoor air filters to keep our indoor air clean. Engineers design drinking water treatment facilities that bring safe drinking water to our schools, offices and homes.

Environmental and civil engineers, in particular, examine and protect the quality of our water resources in many ways. They design water and sewage treatment plants that clean water for human use, and design industrial systems and filters that make sure factory-released water is not polluting our environment. Furthermore, environmental engineers help clean up water sources and air that is polluted. They are challenged to clean the groundwater and then restore it to a natural or usable state so that it remains free from harmful chemicals which could contaminate the drinking water supply and make people sick. Another very important type of engineering involves the creative technologies to dispose of the enormous amount of trash produced in the United States. Engineers design sanitary landfills to prevent groundwater, soil and air pollution. With the mountains of trash winding up in landfills each day, engineers are working to find ways to more quickly break down materials and create methods to reuse what is left out for trash.

Whether keeping our water safe or finding ways to reuse water bottles, engineers are very important to our environmental health. Clearly, engineers greatly contribute to our health and safety.

It is important to take this on board and create lesson plans that align with this big spectrum of environmental studies and nature, and match the curriculum standards.

CHAPTER 14: Latest learning tools in STEM education

As awareness of STEM grows, it continues to evolve and change. Below are some of the latest advancements in STEM education:

1. Created by Leah Buechley, the Lilypad Circuit is a set of electronic pieces which are sewn together and then connected to a power source to create a real working item. Each Lilypad Circuit kit features large conductive sewing tabs and a rounded shape and comprises of three main parts: a power source, conductive paths and pieces to be sewn together. Once constructed, the circuit will light up, giving children the experience of making a working item.

2. As you might guess, Makey Makey is about, erm, making things. With different sections on the website for parents and educators, the Makey shop features a number of weird and wonderful kits for building, creating and inventing.

3. A quick Google search gives you access to hundreds of different projects including music creation and programming, 3D pens and technology, robotics and, one of the latest crazes, e-textiles. For more information on e-textiles and to find out about the Wizkids E-textiles Workshop, visit *wizkidsclub.com/blog*.

4. Programming music. Rhythm makes up a big part of our world – and our now bodies. We walk, breathe and chew in rhythm. Music can be used to great effect in STEM learning. Most children learn an affinity for music from a young age; whether it's the theme tune from a much-loved television program or from a favorite band.

    Helping children to use technology in order to create simple music programs is not only fun but introduces an additional understanding of the world's natural rhythms.

5. 3D pens. Although 3D technology isn't new, the way we use it and harness it is. 3D art pens and filaments allow students to bring their STEM designs to life. Students can be encouraged to set their imagination free in order to create thermoses, balloon rockets, night lights and more.

6. Art bots. Many STEM educators feel that combining art and engineering is a great way to spark girls' interest in STEM subjects. Projects such as the Smart Umbrella allow girls to design their own robot and then to build it. As an open-ended, project-based activity, this has proved to be extremely popular with boys and girls alike.

7. Electronic textiles, also known as smart garments, smart clothing or smart fabrics, are fabrics that incorporate digital components, such as a battery and a light. E-Textiles are of particular interest to young children who delight in wearing garments which light up or make a sound. Making garments out of e-textiles is inexpensive and relatively easy and makes a great STEM project. The Wizkidsclub E-textiles Workshop is the ideal introduction to this fun and STEM-forward technology.

8. 3D printers – In the last few years, 3D printers have been big news for both leisure and educational projects. These clever printers allow students to design and build 3D models and have become so popular that more and more schools and organizations are adding these printers to their equipment.

    There are a number of kits available – *https://www.mystemkits.com/* – which can help to introduce students to simple 3D printing projects.

9. Space – Many children (and adults for that matter) have a fascination with space and this fascination is a great basis for an introduction to STEM. Many space-inspired materials are part of the design and technology curriculum, including shape memory alloys, Kevlar, titanium, Gore-tex, and graphene. The Mission Discovery Space And STEM School summer camp has some great space-inspired projects for children up to 16 years of age.

10. Lighthouse   keeper   challenge Although popular, this one needs a little more planning and requires some financial expenditure. The project is designed to encourage students to work together in order to design a way of transporting lighthouse keepers 200 meters from their lighthouse to the mainland. The students must design a prototype with at least one electronic circuit. Where possible, the project should be completed in one day. *https:// www.stem.org.uk/enrichment/stem-directory/activity/lighthouse-keeper-transfer*

CHAPTER 15: STEM:
Past, present, future

Past: Although the term STEM education was only really introduced in 2001, the principles of teaching hands-on, real-life applications of science, maths, engineering and technology planted its roots much earlier than that. Many believe that, in the 1950s, there was a surge in students taking an interest in these disciplines due to the worldwide space race – as nations competed to be the first (and second and third) into space, a worldwide fascination with space technology was born. In its infancy, S.T.E.A.M and S.T.E.M education methods were designed to introduce a more hands-on, interactive learning experience. From 2001 onwards, more and more schools across the globe began to introduce STEM learning into their curriculum, and this was accelerated further in 2011 when President Barack Obama spoke eloquently about the need to encourage young people to embrace these subjects.

Here and now: As STEM awareness grows, schools are developing mentoring systems and local companies are getting involved by teaming up with schools to educate and inspire their future employees. In fact, the importance of STEM education is now so well recognized that every year, on November 8, America celebrates National STEM/STEAM Day. Although the popularity of STEM learning continues to soar, many countries are now tackling the very real need to encourage more girls and students of an ethnic minority into these professions. Many STEM initiatives aim to address the gender divide of professionals within STEM-related industries. Figures show that, although an impressive 74% of middle school age girls show an interest in engineering, science and mathematics, only around 3% actually choose these subjects as a major when going on to further education.

In terms of employment, STEM industries have fewer women on high-level boards than other kinds of industries – just 12.2% globally in the information technology industry.

A study by the tech giant, Microsoft, has shown that for girls, the interest in STEM subjects peaks in middle school only to drop sharply in high school. As this is a range between the ages of 11 and 15, it's easy to see that social factors are at play here, and so, for parents and educators, this is a problem area that needs to be addressed by working to keep up the momentum of the interest through this sticky growth stage.

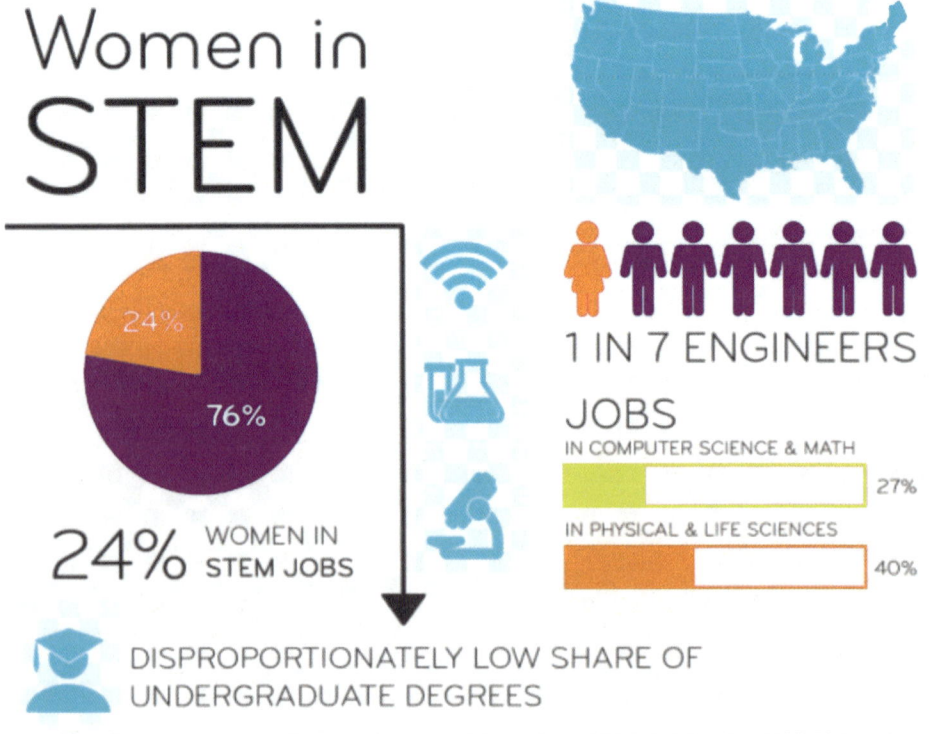

Women in
STEM

24%

76%

24% WOMEN IN STEM JOBS

1 IN 7 ENGINEERS

JOBS
IN COMPUTER SCIENCE & MATH
27%

IN PHYSICAL & LIFE SCIENCES
40%

DISPROPORTIONATELY LOW SHARE OF UNDERGRADUATE DEGREES

In order to become the new wave of leaders and innovators, it's vital that children become passionate about STEM subjects at an early age. Throughout the world, governments are working to make this a reality. Organizations and governments are introducing competitions and events for those students looking to nurture their existing passion for these subjects. Currently available events include the Google Science Fair, eCybermission, and The Ultimate STEM Challenge.

The Ultimate STEM Challenge: STEM Learning runs the Ultimate STEM Challenge for students between the ages of 11 and 14. The challenge offers a choice of three challenges on the theme of sustainability. The 2018 winner of the STEM Challenge was a group of four young UK scientists who produced an energy efficient solution to generate electricity from moving water. The three challenge choices were: (1) Handy Hydro – Create a way to generate electricity from moving water; (2) Parched Plants – Grow indoor plants using a sustainable method which conserves water; (3) Brilliant Biogas – Build a system that generates biomethane from food waste. The all-female group of winners beat over 500 competitors and won an invitation to a celebratory event at The Science Museum and also £500 for their school.

Competitions such as The Ultimate STEM Challenge are a firm step forward in promoting STEM skills in girls – and boys – of all ages.

Future: As STEM becomes an integrated part of education, organizations such as science and technology museums could be persuaded to become an extension of the classroom by serving as hubs for the passionate student.

These days, most of us know someone whose child or grandchild has instructed them in the use of their mobile phone, laptop or tablet. As our world becomes more and more reliant on technology, knowing how it works will become much more vital. In today's world, three-year-old children are using tablets and accessing the internet with impressive proficiency, and these are the people who, in the future, will be inventing the technology that their own children will be using.

Creating a STEM future

As STEM professionals, our role is to educate not just our students but also parents, communities and governments. By getting educators, as well as local businesses, involved, we're creating the next generation of engineers, scientists and technicians. Join the movement on our Facebook page and drop us a line to let us know how you and your school are helping to form our future.

Join the
WIZKIDS CLUB

Enter today and win a FREE BOOK!

Do you have any travel adventure stories or project ideas you want share with me? Yes? Great! You can mail me at my id and become a member of the WIZKIDS CLUB!

www.wizkidsclub.com

Write to me at: sumita@wizkidsclub.com

Made in the USA
Lexington, KY
25 May 2019